LARRY BURKETT

PERSONAL FINANCES

MOODY PRESS
CHICAGO

ISBN: 0-8024-2605-0

2 3 4 5 6 Printing/VP/Year 95 94 93 92 91

Printed in the United States of America

About the Author

Larry Burkett is committed to teaching God's people His principles for managing money. Unfortunately, money management is one area often neglected by Christians, and it is a major cause of conflict and disruption in both business and family life.

For more than two decades Larry has counseled and taught God's principles for finance across the country. As director of Christian Financial Concepts, Larry has counseled, conducted seminars, and written numerous books on the subject of maintaining control of the budget. In additon he is heard on more than 1000 radio outlets worldwide.

Personal Finances

It is important for a Christian to be able to recognize financial bondage, but it is equally important to know how to achieve freedom. Financial freedom manifests itself in every aspect of the Christian's life—relief from worry and tension about overdue bills, a clear conscience before God and man, and the absolute assurance that God is in control of his finances.

That is not to say that a Christian's finances will be totally void of difficulties. Often God allows consequences of earlier actions to reinforce a lesson. But no matter what the circumstances, God promises peace.

When God manages our finances, we have nothing to worry about. He is the master of the universe. It is His wisdom that we seek. Human beings are subject to making a mistake at any moment. But as soon as we admit our error and let God take control

5

again, we are back under His guidance.

Once a Christian truly experiences financial freedom, he or she will never desire to move outside of God's will. Perfect peace is what is promised, and perfect peace is what God delivers.

I have never met a non-Christian who had true freedom from worry, anxiety, tension, harassment, or bitterness about money. Once an individual achieves financial freedom (meaning freedom from the bondage of debts, oppression, envy, covetousness, greed, and resentfulness), he or she stands out like a beacon at sea.

A PRINCIPLE UNDER SCRUTINY

THE CASE FOR PLANNING

Often Christians argue about whether it is biblical to plan. Those who argue against it misunderstand what God says about finances. They argue that God expects us to rely on Him for everything instead of planning. Others create plans so inflexible that they can no longer respond to God's leading. Clearly the answer lies somewhere in between.

God is an orderly provider. The physical world is not chaotic but orderly and well planned. Atoms stay together because God so ordered them. Finances are just another aspect of the Christian's life that God wants to manage. If we are stewards and God is the owner, we must seek His wisdom. Therefore we must go to God's Word for our plans.

BE DIFFERENT

God calls each of us to be disciplined and to sacrifice to accomplish the kingdom's work. Discipline and sacrifice begin with finances, although it is possible to be financially disciplined and still not be an active part of God's work. But it is impossible to be financially undisciplined and be active in God's work. "He who is faithful in a very little thing is faithful also in much; and he who is unrighteous in a very little thing is unrighteous also in much. If therefore you have not been faithful in the use of unrighteous mammon, who will entrust the true riches to you?" (Luke 16:10-11).

Lack of self-discipline affects the spiritual life and manifests itself in inconsistent Bible study and prayer. Without exception, this creates a slackening of spiritual awareness. The place to start being a self-disciplined, servant of the Lord is in our finances.

WHY PLAN?

1. God wants us to be knowledgeable about the assets He has entrusted to us. "Know well the condition of your flocks, and pay attention to your herds" (Proverbs 27:23). For herds or flocks, substitute what you actually have.

2. We are to be an active part of God's plan, exercising our minds and abilities. "Commit your works to the Lord, and your plans will be established" (Proverbs 16:3). We are required to plan and commit.

3. Plan with the future in mind. "For which one of you, when he wants to build a tower, does not first sit down and calculate the cost, to see if he has enough to complete it?" (Luke 14:28). That means we should anticipate the unforeseen.

4. Each Christian should know God's provision for him individually and be content with it. "But godliness actually is a means of great gain, when accompanied by contentment" (1 Timothy 6:6). Accomplishing this requires both husband and wife work-

Larry Burkett

ing and planning together, literally being of "one mind."

WHERE TO START

For those of you who have never —or rarely—developed a financial plan for your family, here are a few basic guidelines. First, if you are married, your plan must involve both husband and wife. At least one full day should be set aside to pray and plan your finances for the year. Second, don't try to do your planning at home where there are innumerable distractions. Find a quiet place where you will not be disturbed. Third, bring all the information you'll need, including last year's bank ledger, budget book, income tax return, checkbook, and so on. Fourth, use a simple but complete family budget guide to help get you started. *The Financial Planning Workbook* and *Debt-Free Living* are resources that give step-by-step instructions for developing a one-year plan and getting out of debt.

DIVIDE DUTIES TO MATCH SKILLS

There should only be one bookkeeper in your home, and it should be the person with the best abilities in

9

that area and the most time available. Usually, the wife makes a better bookkeeper, simply because of attention to detail and time available. However, any plan should be developed by both husband and wife, and they should set aside a specific time at least every other week to jointly discuss progress and problems. If the wife is the bookkeeper, make certain that it is not because the husband refuses to accept his responsibilities to be a leader in the home.

SET GIVING GOALS

But before the budget is established, I counsel Christian couples to establish their giving goals. Why? Because giving should not be motivated by what's left over or what we can "afford" but rather by God's conviction. God's Word tells us to stretch our faith in this area. Usually if a couple can reach an early agreement in this area, the rest of the planning goes easily. *Giving and Tithing* is one resource that may help you decide how and where to do your giving. Since most couples are virtual opposites, one usually wants to give too much and the other too little. The key here is to reach a reasonable compromise while stepping beyond what's safe and truly trusting in God in a material way. "For I testify that according to their ability, and beyond their ability they gave of their own accord" (2 Corinthians 8:3).

PREPARE A PRELIMINARY BUDGET

Once you have determined how much you are to give and the amount of taxes you must pay, you will know your "net spendable income." That is the amount per month that you can spend—but not necessarily what you *should* spend. Each couple must decide before the Lord what portion is theirs to spend each month. For those with sizable net spendable incomes, this question is just as important as how much to give.

The next step in your planning process is to agree upon a preliminary budget. It is preliminary because if you have never lived on a budget before, you will overlook some areas of spending initially. This is particularly true of irregular expenses, such as maintenance. The best way to start is by reviewing each budget category (housing, food, auto, and so on) and establishing what this year's budget will be. A reasonably good guide is to total last year's expenses in each category and then divide the total by twelve. In most cases you will need to add a percentage for inflation.

To establish your budget or spending plan, it will be necessary to go through each category of your budget in this manner. In our budget workbook we use twelve categories: tithe, taxes, housing, food, auto, insurance, debts, entertainment, recreation, clothing, savings, and miscellaneous.

Once you have determined what you should be spending on each category every month, the next step is to monitor your monthly spending. Each budget category should have an account sheet where the budgeted amount is shown. As the money is spent, the balance is reduced, and at the end of the month you will know whether or not you have stuck to your budget.

Two common difficulties often arise in doing financial planning—being too legalistic or being too lax. Trying to correct years of bad financial habits in one month leads to legalism. Both husband and wife must be willing to take equal reductions.

Laxness usually occurs when the budget is planned, filed away, and never monitored. The planning process may make you feel better, but no plan is of value until it is implemented.

How to Plan a Financial Program

DEVELOP A CHANGED ATTITUDE

First you must develop a changed attitude. Generate a plan according to God's conviction, and then utilize it—apply God's principles to your life.

If you make plans that are inflexible, they will only hinder God's work because you won't be able to live with them. Develop plans that guide your financial life but also provide for some recreation and personal enjoyment as well.

BE FLEXIBLE

Do not make plans that are totally dependent on financial increases. God's wisdom can be manifest through a reduction, if necessary, to redirect our lives. We would all be happy to get involved in only profitable ventures. But sometimes God's will is accomplished by a loss instead.

Paul says in Philippians 4:12-13, "I know how to get along with humble means, and I also know how to live in prosperity; in any and every circumstance I have learned the secret of being filled and going hungry, both of having abundance and suffering need. I can do all things through Him who strengthens me." We should have the same perspective in planning.

SOME GUIDELINES

1. Learn to practice patience and moderation in every financial decision.

2. Have a positive attitude.

3. Never get involved in financial decisions that require instant action; allow God to take His course. The difference between a profit and a loss may well be the attitude with which we approach financial investments.

4. Avoid get-rich-quick schemes, no matter how tempting.

5. Maintain your plans for as long as you have peace about them.

6. Do not be inflexible, but don't change your plans just because somebody tells you something different.

The majority of businesses that fail do so because they are undermanaged or undercapitalized; they have inadequate planning. It is futile to operate a business without a cash flow plan (income versus expenses) to allocate resources for paying bills.

God has exactly the same plan for a Christian's home, but unfortunately most of us ignore it. How can anyone manage a home without co-ordinating income and expenses?

SET REALISTIC GOALS

One purpose of planning is to set realistic financial goals as a measuring system to determine if you're on track. A basic goal would be to decide where you want to be financially in one year. If one of your goals is to be debt-free, that's where your plan comes in. Can you realistically reach that goal in one year? If not, how about in two years or three years?

A financial plan for a young couple trying to buy their first home will be totally different from that of a retired couple living on a fixed income. A plan that will work for someone on a regular salary will not function for an athlete whose income may be terminated in the next year. Each plan must be matched to each family. Athletes often use the uncertainty of their income as an excuse for not planning. But that uncertainty is exactly the reason they need to plan even more carefully than the average family. They must learn to live off less than they make and store the surplus during the good years in preparation for the lean years. "Go to the ant, O sluggard, observe her ways and be wise" (Proverbs 6:6).

Every plan must include short-range goals and long-range goals.

SHORT-RANGE GOALS

Short-range plans are those that affect today, and they require our immediate attention. Short-range plans are basically day-by-day occurrences. For example, a housewife must have a short-range plan for buying groceries. It will include how much she buys, how often she buys, and the type of groceries necessary. If she does no planning at all, she has to rush down to the store to buy more groceries before every meal. Likewise, there must be some plan for paying bills. Otherwise, when the paycheck comes, it seems like a windfall. The natural reaction is to spend all the money and ignore the bills that are not due immediately. Later there is no money to meet the obligations. Obviously that is not an adequate plan.

In business short-range plans include such things as what raw materials must be ordered to manufacture the product. If a business did no planning at all, every day the assembly line would have to shut down while someone rushed out to purchase necessary materials. Businesses make goals and develop plans to accomplish them.

Thus, everyone has short-range plans or goals. Some are carefully considered; others are haphazard. If your short-range goal is to make money, you should review it because that is not a Christian objective. Having money as a goal means that you are depending on yourself, not God. The mere ability to make money does not enrich you spiritually (Proverbs 2:4-5). Every Christian who has ever had money as a goal can testify that it does not satisfy. But if your goals are God-directed they will enrich you spiritually and financially. What short-range goals does God desire for us? How can we develop plans to accomplish them?

MAKE YOUR GOALS PERSONAL

Establish your goals in relation to what God asks you to do, not what your neighbor asks you to do. It is easy to get caught up in the frenzy of someone else's schemes. We see others apparently doing well and get talked into jumping into half-baked ideas.

Unfortunately many people who actually like their profession or business feel frustrated because somebody else is making more money in a speculative venture. So they get involved in a program they know little or nothing about. The usual result is a costly financial lesson. There are limitless ways to lose money; one of the best is through bad advice coupled with envy.

STRIVE FOR EXCELLENCE

God wants Christians to excel at whatever we do to the best of our ability. Often Christians rationalize that it is God's plan for us to be second best. So they hang back, never achieving their potential because they fear that others will think them egotistical.

A Christian can excel at whatever he does without egotism. Paul excelled without being egotistical; Simon Peter excelled and remained a humble man. Each knew his source of power, knew what God had asked him to do, and accepted nothing less than excellence. Excellence should be one of our short-range goals.

First Peter 4:11 says, "Whoever speaks, let him speak, as it were, the utterances of God; whoever serves, let him do so as by the strength which God supplies; so that in all things God may be glorified through Jesus Christ." We are to use our abilities for God's glory. For example, it is important that wives and mothers excel at what they do. Usually the mother becomes the teacher of habits in the home; her attitudes are generally reflected by her children. If she excels at what she does and keeps the home well-organized, she can be a great asset to home financial planning.

HONOR GOD IN YOUR WORK

Every Christian should assess the following:

Does my business always exemplify the Christian life?

Does every one of my daily actions witness for Christ?

Can I do my work and honor God?

Does the company I work for deal ethically with others?

Do I help others violate principles that I believe?

Am I providing a genuine service or simply satisfying my own ambitions?

We must each answer those questions if our work is to honor God. For instance, the insurance trade can be a great service. But often it is promoted on the basis of profit for the salesman rather than the needs of the client. So individuals are sold too little insurance at too high a price or too much. Few salesmen provide the quality and quantity of insurance that fit the exact needs of the buyer. It takes more time and effort to do that, but in the end not only will the salesman prosper, but the buyer will become a representative who refers more people to him.

Galatians 6:9 says, "And let us not lose heart in doing good, for in due time we shall reap if we do not grow weary."

LONG-RANGE GOALS

In addition to short-range planning, a Christian needs to assess his long-range goals. Many Christians go through their entire lives without es-

Larry Burkett

tablishing prayerful goals for the use
of their wealth. Many get trapped
into a dogmatic, daily routine. Un-
derstandably, many find themselves
after forty or fifty years of work with
an accumulation of wealth and in a
quandary about what to do with it.
Others find themselves immersed in
problems and financial difficulties
without a prearranged plan of action.
Christians should have long-range financial objectives. Any financial
plan should be in harmony with
prayer-guided long-range goals. Ask
yourself the following questions.

What do I want to achieve in
life?

How am I going to accomplish
God's plan?

If God blesses me with an abundance of money, what will I do with
it? What kind of plan do I have for
such an eventuality?

Not every Christian is wealthy, but
everyone has a responsibility to plan
well, develop good, sound objectives,
and operate according to God's principles. A Christian should establish
long-range goals after personal and
family prayer. The following biblical
principles should be the cornerstone
of every long-range goal.

ACCEPT THE NECESSITY TO PLAN

First, recognize the need to do long-range planning. Like your short-range plans, your long-range plans should be written. Often if you write down what you hope to accomplish, God will provide insight into His plan.

Your long-range goals should reflect your personal financial objectives, a plan for the surplus, and an after-death plan.

SET A MAXIMUM GOAL

A Christian should have a goal of how much he wants to accumulate—the maximum, not minimum. Think in terms of storing for provision rather than storing for protection.

Christians who have minimum financial objectives have not really assessed what's happening to our economy. It is possible that God has asked some Christians to store up for the future needs of others, but the issue again is attitude. Is your attitude one of hoarding or sharing?

When Joseph was in Egypt did he hoard the food that he put aside or did he store it for when it would be needed? Those who do not share in good times certainly will not do so in difficult times.

Once a maximum goal is established, peer approval will cease to be important, and the truth of Proverbs 11:28 will be more apparent: "He who trusts in his riches will fall, but the righteous will flourish like the green leaf."

ESTABLISH A SURPLUS PLAN

You should have a long-range plan for the surplus God supplies. How much will you return to the Lord's work? How much should you supply to your family? How much should you invest? Should you give your children everything they ask for? (Many times, we purchase things for our children instead of spending time with them as a rationalization for our overcommitment to work.) Each Christian must assess for himself God's plan for the surplus. However, God does provide some clear guidelines.

First Corinthians 3:12-13 states, "Now if any man builds upon the foundation with gold, silver, precious stones, wood, hay, straw, each man's work will become evident; for the day will show it, because it is to be revealed with fire; and the fire itself will test the quality of each man's work." What is this work that God refers to? Revelation 2:19 has the answer, "I know your deeds, and your love and faith and service and perseverance, and that your deeds of late are greater than at first." Will Jesus be able to say to you when He returns, "Well done, My good and faithful servant?"

Establish a surplus plan while the opportunity and the capability exist. Do not count on future events to support God's work. If you have money stored and God lays a need on you, give immediately. It may even be necessary to disregard tax advantages. Many people retain investments to take maximum advantage of the tax laws. I don't agree with that "logic"; I'd rather have God as my partner in a venture than the government.

OBEY GOD'S PRINCIPLES

In formulating your long-range plans, pay specific attention to God's principles:

Honesty. Never allow yourself to be trapped into anything that is unethical, immoral, or dishonest, no matter how inviting it seems. Proverbs 16:8 says, "Better is a little with righteousness than great income with injustice." It is important that we observe honesty in all of our plans. There aren't any small lies—just lies. There aren't any small thefts—just thefts.

Employee welfare. Christian employers have an absolute responsibility to care for their employees. Part of your long-range planning in your business should involve the welfare of your employees. If you expect a fair day's work, pay a fair day's wage.

Some company profits belong not only to management but also to the employees. God has a personal management plan in Scripture that would revolutionize business, but often Christian employers are more intent on making money than on providing for the welfare of their employees. First Timothy 5:18 says, "For the Scripture says, 'You shall not muzzle the ox while he is threshing' and 'The laborer is worthy of his wages.'" Christian employers have not only additional authority but additional responsibility as well.

Concern for others. Opportunities to take advantage of others will arise. You must precondition your attitude to avoid temptation. "Do not rob the poor because he is poor, or crush the afflicted at the gate; for the Lord will plead their case, and take the life of those who rob them" (Proverbs 22:22-23).

Obey the law. God demands obedience to the law in your long-range plans. I speak here specifically of tax laws. There are two terms used to describe tax planning. One is tax avoidance, which is taking all the legal remedies available under the law; the other is tax evasion, which is taking all the legal remedies plus some not allowed within the boundaries of the law. The line between the two is thin and easily crossed.

I find that many Christians rationalize their violation of tax laws. People who would not think of robbing a bank justify stealing from the government. On the one hand I object to the highly lopsided tax structure of our system, but to illegally avoid the debt due is stealing. It is easy to rationalize because the government is a large, inflexible institution, but it is still stealing.

Proverbs 15:27 states, "He who profits illicitly troubles his own house, but he who hates bribes will live." Take maximum advantage of every tax law in existence: charitable giving, tax sheltering, depreciation, and expenses, but be careful not to cross the line and become involved in tax evasion and theft.

Every Christian must establish a long-range family plan. What do you want for your family? Have you ever brought your family together to pray about how God wants you to live?

God cares about the house you live in, the car you drive, where you work, whether your wife should work, your children's college, and even the food you eat. Have you ever prayed about those things? If you haven't, how can you expect to know what God's will is for your family is?

Can you ever store enough to protect your family? I don't believe so. The best you can do is short-term provision. God has a better plan for every Christian who seeks His wisdom. When God says, "Be not anxious," that does not mean to be unconcerned or imprudent. There is a distinct difference between concern or preparedness and worry.

Establish priorities. Your long-range goals should focus on financial priorities. There is a vast difference between needs, wants, and desires. Needs are the purchases necessary to provide your basic requirements such as food, clothing, a job, home, medical coverage, and others. "And if we have food and covering, with these we shall be content" (1 Timothy 6:8).

Wants involve choices about the quality of goods to be used: dress clothes versus work clothes, steak versus hamburger, a new car versus a used car, and so on. 1 Peter 3:3-4 gives a point of reference for determining wants in a Christian's life: "And let not your adornment be merely external—braiding the hair, and wearing gold jewelry, or putting on dresses; but let it be the hidden person of the heart, with the imperishable quality of a gentle and quiet spirit, which is precious in the sight of God."

Desires are choices that should be made only out of surplus funds after all other obligations have been met.

Establish priorities with your family, particularly your children. Help them understand the difference between a need, a want, and a desire. When your child approaches you with a request, discuss which category it falls under.

If it is a need, it should be supplied. But if it is a want or a desire, you should be able to establish the fact that if he or she wants it, perhaps your child should earn it. When a child learns that he must earn some of his wants and desires, he makes a quick adjustment. Comic books are weighed against the value of a new baseball bat, a nonsense toy against a coin for his collection.

Be consistent and fair but firm. Just as God will not grant us whims that work to our detriment, so you must hold the same position with your children.

Have a family giving plan. Why should God trust you with a surplus? Does your family manage money well? Do your children understand a proper attitude about material possessions? What plans do the other members of your family have for the money they earn? Are they willing to tithe openly and willingly without your pressuring them? Bring them into the decision, and pray as a family.

Have an estate plan. Do you have a plan for how much to leave your family after your death? Is it based on provision or protection? You need to realize that you cannot protect your family. Those who store up great amounts of life insurance seeking after-death protection for their families are fooling themselves. We attempt to build great walled cities around our families because we believe it is necessary to protect them against every possibility. But there is a better way. God's plan will revolutionize our concept of protection. *Insurance Plans* is a booklet that examines a practical ways to establish an estate or inheritance plan.

Have a contingency plan. A Christian must establish a contingency plan in the event that he accumulates wealth faster than anticipated. Scripture is clear on this point; God's surplus is to be shared. In Proverbs 11:24-25 we find, "There is one who scatters, yet increases all the more, and there is one who withholds what is justly due, but it results only in want. The generous man will be prosperous, and he who waters will himself be watered." That is God's plan for Christians, but unless one has a predetermined plan for increase, expenses will be adjusted to offset any increases. Consequently, there will never be a surplus to share.

Larry Burkett

STEPS TO FINANCIAL FREEDOM

How can we achieve financial freedom? According to God's plan, what must we do?

TRANSFER OWNERSHIP

A Christian must transfer owner-ship of every possession to God. That means his money, time, family, ma-terial possessions, education, even earning potential for the future. Do-ing so is essential to experiencing the Spirit-filled life in his finances.

A Christian must realize that there is absolutely no substitute for this step. If you believe that you are the owner of even a single possession, anything affecting that possession will affect your attitude. God will not input His perfect will into our lives unless we first surrender our will to Him.

If, however, we make a total transfer of everything to God, He will demonstrate His ability. It is impor-tant to understand and accept God's conditions for His control (Deuteron-omy 5:32-33). God will keep His prom-ise to provide every need we have through physical, material, and spir-itual means.

31

It is simple to say, "I make total transfer of everything to God," but it is not simple to do. At first, it is difficult to consistently seek God's will in the area of material things because we are so accustomed to self-management and control.

What a great relief it is to turn our burdens over to Him. Then if something happens to the car, you can say, "Father, I gave this car to You; I've maintained it to the best of my ability, but I don't own it. It belongs to You, so do with it whatever You would like." Then look for God's blessing.

ACHIEVE FREEDOM FROM DEBT

A Christian must get out of debt altogether. Debt exists with any of the following conditions: Payment is past due for money, goods, or services that are owed to other people. The total value of unsecured liabilities exceeds total assets. In other words, if you had to cash out at any time, there would be a negative balance on your account.

Following are six steps to becoming free from debt:

1. Have a written plan. A written plan is an absolute necessity for ev-

eryone in financial bondage. Write
out a plan of all expenditures in order of importance. The order of importance is crucial because we forget
the difference between needs, wants,
and desires. First John 2:15-16 says,
"Do not love the world, nor the things
in the world. If anyone loves the
world, the love of the Father is not in
him. For all that is in the world, the
lust of the flesh and the lust of the
eyes and the boastful pride of life, is
not from the Father, but is from the
world."

2. Limit expenditures to essentials.
A Christian in debt must stop any expenditure that is not absolutely essential (Proverbs 21:17). Look for
services around the home that can be
done without outside cost. Also begin
to develop some home skills. By uti-
lizing your own skills, you can cut
down on expenditures that are not
essential.

What I'm expressing is an attitude of conservatism. Remember that
many expenditures are assumed to be
essential only because of our society.
Fifty years ago almost all the labor
supplied in the home was through family members—not professionals who
charged for it.

Christians who are in bondage must begin to assess what they can do for themselves and stop frivolities.

3. *Think before buying.* A Christian who is in debt (and even those who aren't) should think before every purchase (Proverbs 24:3). Evaluate your purchases as follows:

Is it a necessity? Have I assessed whether it is a need, a want, or a desire?

Does the purchase reflect my Christian ethics? (For example, *Playboy* obviously does not reflect Christian ethics.) Can I continue to subscribe to magazines, encyclopedias, or book and tape clubs while I owe others?

Is this the best possible buy, or am I purchasing only because I have this credit card?

Is it a highly depreciative item? (Swimming pools, boats, and sports cars all fall into this category.)

Does it require costly upkeep? (Many items fall within this category—mobile homes, swimming pools, color television sets.)

4. *Discontinue credit buying.* A Christian in debt should buy on a cash basis only. Often an individual in debt with an asset that can be converted into cash asks, "Would it be

better to sell this asset and pay off the debts?" That is a possible option but it is only wise if he or she first learns new spending habits. Otherwise it treats the symptom rather than the problem.

For example, I remember a couple who were in dire financial bondage to credit card debts. They owed more than $20,000 and paid in excess of $4,000 a year in interest alone. As I helped them in their planning, it seemed reasonable to sell their home and apply the money to their debts, which would have paid them off. They did so, but less than a year later they were back in debt, owing about $6,000 in credit card debts and without a home this time.

What happened? I had treated a symptom rather than the problem. The problem was their irresponsible attitude about credit cards. Without working out a plan to discontinue using the cards, they fell back into the same trap. As soon as they needed something and lacked the cash to purchase it, out came the card.

The principle to observe is this: If you are in debt from the misuse of credit, stop—totally stop—using it. One of the best things to do with credit cards is to preheat the oven to

400 degrees and put them in it. Then mail the cards back to their respective companies and tell them not to mail you any more. Include in your letter the plan for paying that credit card debt, and commit yourself to buying solely on a cash basis. For more help in developing good habits to get out of debt refer to *Financial Freedom*.

Once good habits have been developed and the bondage from the misuse of credit cards has been broken, evaluate the feasibility of converting assets to pay off debts. At that point you won't simply be treating the symptom.

5. *Avoid leverage.* When in debt, avoid the use of what is called "leverage." For example, if you bought a piece of property that cost $10,000 and put $1,000 down, that represents a nine to one lever. You have invested 10 percent of your money and borrowed 90 percent.

Borrowing money to invest is not a scriptural principle. When you borrow money from a bank to make an investment, your repaying the bank loan is dependent on the investment's making a profit. But if a profit is not made and you can't make the payments, you lose the investment and still owe the bank.

6. *Practice saving.* A Christian should practice saving money on a regular basis. That includes those who are in debt. Even if you can only save $5 a month, develop a discipline of saving.

That does not mean you should store up a large amount of money while failing to pay your creditors, but one of the best habits a young couple can develop is saving a small amount on a regular basis.

Everyone in our society who lives above the poverty level has the capability to save money, but many fail to do so because they believe that the amount they can save is so small it's meaningless. Others believe that God frowns upon a Christian's saving anything. Neither of those two attitudes is scriptural. "There is precious treasure and oil in the dwelling of the wise, but a foolish man swallows it up" (Proverbs 21:20). The Bible instructs us to save on a regular basis.

ESTABLISH THE TITHE

Every Christian should establish the tithe as the minimum testimony to God's ownership. Through giving we bring His power in finances into focus. God always wants us to give the first part to Him, but He also wants us to pay our creditors. That requires establishing a plan and probably making sacrifices until all debts are current.

You cannot sacrifice God's part —that is not your prerogative as a Christian. "Now this I say, he who sows sparingly shall also reap sparingly; and he who sows bountifully shall also reap bountifully" (2 Corinthians 9:6). So what is the key? If a sacrifice is necessary—and it almost always is—do not sacrifice God's or your creditor's share. Choose a portion of your own expenditures to sacrifice.

ACCEPT GOD'S PROVISION

To obtain financial peace, recognize and accept that God's provision is used to direct each of our lives. Often Christians lose sight of the fact that God's will can be accomplished by withholding funds; we tend to think He can direct us only by abundance. But God does not choose for everyone to live in prosperity. As stated before, that does not mean we must live in poverty, but it may mean

that God want us to be more respon-
sive to His day-by-day control.

Each Christian must learn to live
on what God provides and not suc-
cumb to the pressure brought on by
driving desires for wealth and material things.

DEVELOP A CLEAR CONSCIENCE

A Christian must have a clear
conscience regarding past business
practices and personal dealings. That
may require restitution in addition
to a changed attitude.

I recall a friend who had
wronged an individual financially
before he became a Christian. God
convicted him and indicated that he
should go and make restitution. He
contacted the individual, confessed
what he had done, and offered to
make it right. The person refused to
forgive and wouldn't take any money.

At first it hurt my friend's ego
and pride—until he realized that it
was not for the offended person that
he had confessed, but for himself. He
did not offer restitution primarily to
pay back the loss but to restore his
relationship with God. God had for-
given him, and he had done exactly

what God had asked. Nothing further was required.

PUT OTHERS FIRST

A Christian seeking financial freedom must always be willing to put other people first. That does not mean a Christian has to be a floor mat for others; it simply means that he doesn't profit at the disadvantage of someone else.

LIMIT TIME INVOLVEMENT

A Christian must also limit time devoted to business affairs when his or her family suffers. "Do not weary yourself to gain wealth, cease from your consideration of it. When you set your eyes on it, it is gone. For wealth certainly makes itself wings, like an eagle that flies toward the heavens" (Proverbs 23:4-5). Many Christians are trapped in the cycle of overcommitment to business or money pursuits.

The first priority in a Christian's life is to develop his personal relationship with Jesus Christ.

The second priority is a commitment to his family, which includes teaching them God's Word. This training means a specific time commit-

Larry Burkett

ment. Sacrifice if necessary. If you find that your family time together works best between eight and nine in the evening, commit that time to God. Turn off the television, have the children do their homework early, and begin to study the Bible together. It is important for the whole family to worship God and pray together.

The third priority in a Christian's life should be church activities, social groups, work, and other hobbies he might have.

AVOID INDULGENCE

To achieve financial freedom every Christian must avoid the indulgences of life.

The range in which God's will can be found is between Luke 9:23 where Christ says, "If anyone wishes to come after Me, let him deny himself, and take up his cross daily, and follow Me," and John 6:27, "Do not work for the food which perishes, but for the food which endures to eternal life, which the Son of Man shall give to you, for on Him the Father, even God, has set His seal."

Does your lifestyle fit within this range? Are you willing to trust God and deny yourself some indulgences?

41

As you do, He will supply you even more. Unfortunately most of us are self-indulgent, rarely denying our own wants or desires. Most of us can reduce our expenditures substantially without a real reduction in living standard.

SEEK CHRISTIAN COUNSELING

It is important to seek good Christian counseling whenever in doubt. "Without consultation, plans are frustrated, but with many counselors they succeed" (Proverbs 15:22). God admonishes us to seek counsel and not rely solely on our own resources. In financial planning many Christians become frustrated because they lack necessary knowledge, and they give up. God has supplied others with the ability to help in the area of finances. Seek them out.

STEPS TO MAKING A BUDGET

The following is provided as a practical guide to help you establish a family budget. A sample budgeting form is shown on pages 56-57. Use this form to guide your budget preparation.

STEP 1—LIST MONTHLY EXPENDITURES

A. Fixed Expenses
  1. Tithe
  2. Federal income taxes (if taxes are deducted, ignore this item)
  3. State income taxes (if taxes are deducted, ignore this item)
  4. Federal social security taxes (if taxes are deducted, ignore this item)
  5. Housing expenses (payment/rent)
  6. Residence taxes
  7. Residence insurance
  8. Other
B. Variable Expenses
  1. Food
  2. Outstanding debts
  3. Utilities
  4. Insurance (life, health, auto)
  5. Entertainment, recreation
  6. Clothing allowance
  7. Medical/dental
  8. Savings
  9. Miscellaneous

Note: In order to accurately determine variable expenses, it is suggested that both husband and wife keep an expense diary for thirty days. List every expenditure, even twenty-five-cent purchases.

STEP 2—LIST AVAILABLE
INCOME PER MONTH

1. Salary
2. Rents
3. Notes
4. Interest
5. Dividends
6. Income tax refunds
7. Other

Note: If you operate on a non-fixed monthly income, use a yearly average divided into months.

STEP 3—COMPARE INCOME
VERSUS EXPENSES

If total income exceeds total expenses, you have only to implement a method of budget control in your home. If, however, expenses exceed income (or more stringent controls in spending are desired), additional steps are necessary. In that case, an analysis of each budget area is necessary.

BUDGET BUSTERS

"Budget busters" are the potential problem areas that can ruin a budget. Failure to control even one of these areas can result in financial disaster in the home. This area is evaluated by typical budget percentages for a $25,000 income. Naturally, these percentages will vary with income and location.

HOUSING (38 PERCENT OF NET INCOME)

Typically, housing is one of the largest home budget problems. Many families buy a home they can't afford. It is not necessary for everyone to own a home. The decision to buy or rent should be based on needs and financial ability rather than internal or external pressure. *Major Purchases* explains how to decide whether to buy or rent your home.

FOOD (12 PERCENT OF NET INCOME)

Many families buy too much food. Others buy too little. Typically, the average American family buys the wrong type of food. The reduction of a family's food bill requires quantity and quality planning.

Hints for grocery shopping
Always use a written list.
Conserve gas by buying food for a longer period and in larger quantities.

Avoid buying when hungry (especially if you're a "sugarholic").

Use a calculator, if possible, to total purchases.

Reduce or eliminate paper products—plates, cups, napkins, and so on. Use cloth napkins.

Evaluate where to purchase sundry items such as shampoo and toothpaste. These are normally somewhat cheaper at chain drugstore sales.

Avoid processed and sugar-coated cereals. They are expensive and have little nutritional value.

Avoid prepared foods such as TV dinners, pot pies, and cakes. You are paying for labor that you can do yourself.

Determine good meat cuts that are available from roasts or shoulders, and have the butcher cut them for you. Buying steaks by the package on sales is fairly inexpensive also.

Try house-brand canned products. They are normally cheaper and just as nutritious.

Avoid products in a cyclical price hike. Substitute or eliminate.

Shop for advertised specials.

Avoid stores that give merchandise stamps if their prices reflect the cost of the stamps. (Not all do—some simply substitute stamps for other advertising.)

Purchase milk, bread, eggs, and so on from specialty outlet stores if possible. Prices are usually 10 to 15 percent lower. Keep some dry milk on hand to reduce "quick" trips to the store.

Avoid buying non-grocery items in a supermarket except on sale. They are normally high markup items.

Use normal foods processed through a blender for baby foods.

Leave the children at home to avoid unnecessary pressure.

Check every item as it is being rung up at the store and again when you get home.

Can fresh vegetables whenever possible. Make bulk purchases with other families at farmers' markets and such. Note: Secure canning supplies during off seasons.

AUTOMOBILES
(15 PERCENT OF NET INCOME)

Often we are unwise in our decision-making when it come to our machines—especially our cars. Those who buy a new car, keep it for less than four years, and then trade it for a new model waste the maximum amount of money. Some people, such as salesmen who drive a great deal, need new cars frequently; most of us do not.

DEBTS (5 PERCENT OF NET INCOME)

Ideally, a budget should need 7 percent or less to pay debts. Unfortunately, the norm in American families is far in excess of this amount. What can you do if this situation exists?

1. Destroy all of your credit cards.
2. Establish a payment schedule that includes all creditors.
3. Contact all creditors, honestly relate your problems, and arrange an equitable repayment plan.
4. Buy on a cash basis, and sacrifice your wants and desires until you are current.

INSURANCE (5 PERCENT OF NET INCOME)

Few people understand insurance —how much is needed or what kind is necessary. Almost no one would allow someone to sell him a Rolls Royce when he could afford only a Chevrolet; yet many purchase high-cost insurance when their needs dictate otherwise.

Insurance should be used as supplementary provision for the family, not protection or profit. An insurance plan is not designed for saving money or for retirement.

In our society insurance can be used as an inexpensive vehicle to provide future family income and thus release funds today for family use and the Lord's work. Purchased in excess, however, insurance can put a family in debt, steal the Lord's money, and encourage dependence on the world.

One of your best insurance assets is to have a trustworthy agent in charge of your program. A good insurance agent can select from several different companies to provide you with the best possible buy and can create a brief, uncomplicated plan to analyze your exact needs. *Insurance Plans* discusses different insurance options and how to tell what you really need.

RECREATION-ENTERTAINMENT
(5 PERCENT OF NET INCOME)

Recreation is not bad if put in the proper perspective. But we are a recreation-oriented society, and if you are in debt you should not use your creditor's money to entertain yourself.

What a terrible witness it is for a Christian who is already in financial bondage to indulge himself at the expense of others. God knows we need rest and relaxation, and He often provides it from unexpected sources once our attitude is correct. Every believer, whether in debt or not, should probably reduce entertainment expenses. This can usually be done without sacrificing quality family time.

Recreation hints

Plan vacations during off seasons if possible.

Consider a camping vacation to avoid motel and food expenses. Christian friends can pool the expenses of camping items.

Select vacation areas in your general locale.

Consider swapping residences with a Christian family in another locale to provide an inexpensive vacation.

Play family games in place of movies.

Consider taking trips with another family to reduce expenses.

If flying, use the least expensive coach fare (i.e., flying late at night or in early morning usually saves 10 to 20 percent).

Larry Burkett

CLOTHING (5 PERCENT OF NET INCOME)

Many families in debt sacrifice the clothing area of their budget because of excesses in other areas. Yet with prudent planning and buying your family can be clothed neatly without great expense:

1. Save enough money to buy without using credit.
2. Educate family members on clothing care.
3. Apply discipline with children to enforce these habits.
4. Develop skills in making and mending clothing.

Learn to utilize your resources rather than be a consumer. How many families have closets full of clothes they no longer wear because they are "out of style"?

Many families with large surplus incomes spend excessively in the area of clothing. Assess whether it really matters that you have all of the latest styles. Do you buy clothes to satisfy a need or a desire?

Clothing hints

Make as many of your children's clothes as time will allow. Your average savings will be 50 to 60 percent.

List clothing needs and purchase as much as possible during the "off" season.

Select outfits that can be mixed and used in multiple combinations.

Frequent discount outlets that carry unmarked name-brand goods.

Frequent factory outlet stores for closeout values of top quality.

Select washable fabrics in new clothes.

Use coin-operated dry cleaning machines instead of commercial cleaners.

Practice early repair for damaged clothing.

Learn to utilize all clothing fully, especially children's wear.

MEDICAL/DENTAL
(5 PERCENT OF NET INCOME)

You must anticipate these expenses in your budget and set aside funds regularly; failure to do so will wreck your plans and lead to indebtedness. Do not sacrifice family health due to lack of planning, but at the same time do not use doctors excessively. Proper prevention is much cheaper than correction. You can avoid many dental bills by teaching children to eat the right foods and clean their teeth properly. Your dentist will supply all the information you need on this subject. Many doctor bills can be avoided in the same way. Take proper care of your body through diet, rest, and exercise, and it will respond with good health. Abuse your body, and you must ultimately pay through illnesses. That is not to say that all illnesses or problems are caused by neglect, but a great many are.

Do not hesitate to question doctors and dentists in advance about costs. Educate yourself enough to discern when you are getting a good value for your money. Most ethical professionals will not take offense at your questions. If they do, that may be a hint to change services.

When filling prescriptions, shop around. You will be amazed to discover the wide variance in prices from one store to the next. Ask about cash discounts, too. Many stores will give 5 to 10 percent off for cash purchases.

SAVINGS (5 PERCENT OF NET INCOME)

It is important to build some savings into your budget. Otherwise, the use of credit becomes a lifelong necessity and debt a way of life. Your savings will allow you to purchase items for cash and shop for the best buys, irrespective of the store.

Saving hints

Use a company payroll withdrawal, if possible. It removes the money before you receive it.

Use an automatic bank withdrawal from your checking account.

Write a check to your savings account as if it were a creditor.

When an existing debt is paid off, reallocate that money to savings.

VARIABLE HOUSEHOLD EXPENSES
(MISCELLANEOUS)
(5 PERCENT OF NET INCOME)

Some expenses occur monthly, whereas others occur on an as-needed basis (such as appliances).

One of the most important factors in home expenses is you. If you can perform routine maintenance and repair, considerable expense can be avoided. A part of care and maintenance around the home relates to family life, particularly the training of children. When they see Mom and Dad willing to do some physical labor around the home, they will learn good habits.

Larry Burkett

Some men avoid working on home projects because they say they lack the necessary skills. But skills are learned, not gifted. There are many good books that detail every area of home maintenance.

Living on a budget is not only prudent, but it can be fun. As you have successes in various areas, share them with others. Challenge your children as well.

You now have the necessary tools to establish a budget. The rest is up to you. God's blessing rests upon those who live "properly and in an orderly manner" (1 Corinthians 14:40).

The Family Budget Guide
(Monthly Income and Expenses)

INCOME PER MONTH   _____
  Salary   _____
  Interest   _____
  Dividends   _____
  Notes   _____
  Rents   _____
  TOTAL GROSS INCOME   _____

Less:
1. Tithe   _____
2. Tax   _____
  NET SPENDABLE INCOME   _____
3. Housing 38%*
      Mortgage (rent)   _____
      Insurance   _____
      Taxes   _____
      Electricity   _____
      Gas   _____
      Water   _____
      Sanitation   _____
      Telephone   _____
      Maintenance   _____
      Other   _____
4. Food 12%   _____
5. Automobile(s) 15%   _____
      Payments   _____
      Gas and Oil   _____
      Insurance   _____
      License   _____
      Taxes   _____
      Maintenance/Repair/
        Replacement   _____
6. Insurance 5%   _____
      Life   _____
      Medical   _____
      Other   _____
7. Debts 5%   _____
      Credit Card   _____
      Loans and Notes   _____
      Other   _____

* Percentages based on a $25,000 gross annual income.

8. Entertainment and
   Recreation 5%   _____
9. Clothing 5%   _____
10. Savings 5%   _____
11. Medical Expenses 5%   _____
    Doctor   _____
12. Miscellaneous 5%   _____
    Toiletry, Cosmetics   _____
    Beauty, Barber   _____
    Laundry, Cleaning   _____
    Allowances, Lunches   _____
    Subscriptions   _____
    Gifts (incl. Christmas) _____
    Special education   _____
    Cash   _____
    Other   _____
13. School/Child Care 10%   _____
    (If you use this budget cate-
    gory, the percentages of the
    other categories must be re-
    duced by an equal amount.)
    TOTAL EXPENSES   _____

INCOME VERSUS EXPENSE
   Net Spendable Income   _____
   Less Expenses   _____
   Total (Deficit/Surplus)   _____

FORM 1

The bottom line total should break even or show a surplus. If total expenses are greater than net spendable income, you must cut back on expenses. The percentages for fixed and variable expenses may be adjusted, but your total should not exceed your net spendable income.

Variable Expense Planning

Planning for those expenses that are not paid on a regular monthly basis, by estimating the yearly cost and determining the monthly amount needed to be set aside for that expense. A helpful formula is to allow the previous year's expense and add 5 percent.

	Estimated Cost	Per Month
1. VACATION	$_____ ÷ 12 =	$_____
2. DENTIST	$_____ ÷ 12 =	$_____
3. DOCTOR	$_____ ÷ 12 =	$_____
4. AUTOMOBILE	$_____ ÷ 12 =	$_____
5. ANNUAL INSURANCE	$_____ ÷ 12 =	$_____
(Life)	$_____ ÷ 12 =	$_____
(Health)	$_____ ÷ 12 =	$_____
(Auto)	$_____ ÷ 12 =	$_____
(Home)	$_____ ÷ 12 =	$_____
6. CLOTHING	$_____ ÷ 12 =	$_____
7. INVESTMENTS	$_____ ÷ 12 =	$_____
8. OTHER	$_____ ÷ 12 =	$_____
	$_____ ÷ 12 =	$_____

FORM 2

Budget Percentage Guidelines

SALARY FOR GUIDELINE = _____/year

GROSS INCOME PER MONTH _____

Tithe	(10% of Gross)	(_____)	=	$_____
Tax	(12% of Gross)	(_____)	=	$_____
NET SPENDABLE INCOME		(_____)		
Housing	(32% of Net)	(_____)	=	$_____
Food	(15% of Net)	(_____)	=	_____
Auto	(15% of Net)	(_____)	=	_____
Insurance	(5% of Net)	(_____)	=	_____
Debts	(5% of Net)	(_____)	=	_____
Entertain. & Rec.	(7% of Net)	(_____)	=	_____
Clothing	(5% of Net)	(_____)	=	_____
Savings	(5% of Net)	(_____)	=	_____
Medical/ Dental	(5% of Net)	(_____)	=	_____
Miscellaneous	(6% of Net)	(_____)	=	_____

TOTAL (Cannot Exceed Net Spendable Income) $_____

FORM 3

Budget Percentage Guidelines
(sample filled in)

Salary for Guideline = $15,000 /year

Gross Income Per month $1,250

Tithe	(10% of Gross)	(1250)	= $	125
Tax	(12% of Gross)	(1250)	= $	150
Net Spendable Income		975		
Housing	(32% of Net)	(975)	= $	312
Food	(15% of Net)	(975)	=	146
Auto	(15% of Net)	(975)	=	146
Insurance	(5% of Net)	(975)	=	49
Debts	(5% of Net)	(975)	=	49
Entertain. & Rec.	(7% of Net)	(975)	=	68
Clothing	(5% of Net)	(975)	=	49
Savings	(5% of Net)	(975)	=	49
Medical	(5% of Net)	(975)	=	49
Miscellaneous	(6% of Net)	(975)	=	58
Total	(Cannot exceed Net Spendable Income)		$	975

FIGURE 1

Percentage Guide for Family Income

Gross Income	15,000	20,000	40,000	50,000	60,000
Tithe	10%	10%	10%	10%	10%
Taxes	12%	14%	15%	17%	21%
NET SPENDABLE	11,700	15,200	30,000	36,500	41,400
Housing	32%	30%	28%	25%	25%
Auto	15%	15%	12%	12%	12%
Food	15%	16%	14%	14%	10%
Insurance	5%	5%	5%	5%	5%
Entertainment/Rec.	7%	7%	7%	7%	7%
Clothing	5%	5%	5%	6%	6%
Medical/Dental	5%	5%	4%	4%	4%
Miscellaneous	6%	7%	7%	8%	8%
Savings	5%	5%	5%	5%	5%
Debts	5%	5%	5%	5%	5%
Investments	—	—	8%	9%	13%

FIGURE 2

Budget Analysis

Per Year ___15,000___ Net Spendable Income Per Month ___938___

Per Month ___1,250___

MONTHLY PAYMENT CATEGORY	EXISTING BUDGET	MONTHLY GUIDELINE BUDGET	DIFFERENCE + OR −	NEW MONTHLY BUDGET
1. Tithe				
2. Taxes				
NET SPENDABLE INCOME (PER MONTH)	$	$	$	$
3. Housing				
4. Food				
5. Automobile(s)				
6. Insurance				
7. Debts				
8. Enter. & Recreation				
9. Clothing				
10. Savings				
11. Medical				
12. Miscellaneous				
TOTALS (Items 3 through 12)	$	$	/////////	$

FORM 4

Budget Analysis
(sample filled in)

PER YEAR _____   NET SPENDABLE INCOME PER MONTH _____

PER MONTH _____

MONTHLY PAYMENT CATEGORY	EXISTING BUDGET	MONTHLY GUIDELINE BUDGET	DIFFERENCE + OR –	NEW MONTHLY BUDGET
1. Tithe	125	125	0	125
2. Taxes	187	150	+37	150
NET SPENDABLE INCOME (Per Month)	$ 938	$ 975	$ +37	$ 975
3. Housing	391	312	– 75	380
4. Food	230	146	– 84	200
5. Automobile(s)	85	146	+61	85
6. Insurance	39	49	+10	39
7. Debts	90	49	–41	75
8. Enter. & Recreation	53	68	+15	40
9. Clothing	50	49	–1	35
10. Savings	0	49	+49	40
11. Medical	30	49	+19	25
12. Miscellaneous	69	58	–11	56
TOTALS (Items 3 through 12)	$ 1037	$ 975		$ 975

FIGURE 3

Income Allocation

INCOME		INCOME SOURCE/PAY PERIOD			
BUDGET CATEGORY	MONTHLY ALLOCATION				
1. TITHE					
2. TAX					
3. HOUSING					
4. FOOD					
5. AUTO					
6. INSURANCE					
7. DEBTS					
8. ENTERTAINMENT & RECREATION					
9. CLOTHING					
10. SAVINGS					
11. MEDICAL/DENTAL					
12. MISCELLANEOUS					

FORM 5

List of Debts

TO WHOM OWED	CONTACT NAME PHONE NO.	PAY OFF	PAYMENTS LEFT	MONTHLY PAYMENT	DATE

Form 6

Practical Applications

A friend once told me that information without application leads to frustration. To help avoid that problem, this section provides ideas to help you apply God's principles of finances.

FAMILY COMMUNICATION GOALS

Communication is vital to family financial planning. To enhance communication, some questions are listed for both husband and wife. I suggest that each of you do them separately. Write down every answer as if your spouse were asking the question. Then, during a time when you won't be interrupted, evaluate your answers together.

The questions are intended to enrich the discussions of mature, communicating Christian couples. Use them as tools of love, not ammunition for war.

Personal Finances

A. Personal Goals

To be answered as if your husband/wife were asking:

1. What are your personal goals in life?

   _____

2. What personal goals have you set for this coming year?

   _____

3. How can I help you achieve your goals?

   _____

4. What can I do to help or improve our financial situation?

   _____

5. Do you think there is a proper balance between my outside activity and my time at home?

   _____

6. Would you like me to do more things around the house such as cleaning and decorating?

   _____

7. In regard to my activities outside the home, what would you consider my priorities?

   _____

8. Do you think I need to improve in any area, such as my appearance, manners, and attitudes?

_____

B. Marriage Goals

1. Do you believe our marriage is maturing and we are coming closer together?

_____

2. Do you think we communicate clearly?

_____

3. Am I sensitive to your personal needs?

_____

4. What would you like me to say or do the next time you seem to be angry with me or you are not speaking to me?

_____

5. The next time you are late in getting ready to go someplace, what would you like me to say or do?

_____

6. What would you like me to say or do the next time you seem to

be getting impatient with something or someone?

_____

7. What would you like me to say or do if you begin to criticize someone?

_____

8. Do you think I need to improve in getting ready on time or getting to meetings on time?

_____

9. Do you think we should go out together more often?

_____

10. Do I make cutting remarks about you or criticize you in front of other people?

_____

11. What should I do in public to encourage you?

_____

12. Do I respond to your suggestions and ideas as if I had already thought of them instead of thanking you and encouraging you to contribute more?

_____

13. Do I tell you enough about what I do every day?

    _____

14. What little acts of love do I do for you?

    _____

15. What most often causes you to get angry with me?

    _____

16. Do I convey my admiration and respect for you often enough?

    _____

17. Do we pretend a happy marriage in front of other people?

    _____

18. What do you think 1 Corinthians 7:3-7 means?

    _____

19. Do you think we need to see a marriage counselor?

    _____

20. What are the responsibilities of a "helpmate"?

    _____

21. Do we give each other the same attention we did before we had children?

    _____

C. Family Goals
   1. What are our family goals?

   _____

   2. Are we achieving our family goals?

   _____

   3. (wife) What can I do to help you fulfill your responsibilities as spiritual leader of our family?

   _____

   (husband) How can I better fulfill my responsibilities as spiritual leader?

   _____

   4. Do you think we meet the spiritual needs of our family?

   _____

   5. What kinds of family devotions should we have?

   _____

   6. List the responsibilities stated for the husband and wife in the following passages:

   1 Peter 3:1-2 _____

   Colossians 3:18-19 _____

   1 Timothy 2:11-15 _____

   1 Corinthians 11:3 _____

   Ephesians 5:17-33 _____

7. Do you think we have a consistent prayer life together?

_____

8. Do you think we are adequately involved in our local church?

_____

9. Do you think we are meeting the physical needs of our family?

_____

10. Should we improve our eating habits?

_____

11. Should we get more exercise?

_____

12. Do we make good use of our time? For example, do we watch too much TV? Should we have more hobbies? Read more?

_____

13. How and when should we discipline our children? What do you think is the biblical viewpoint of discipline?

_____

14. List the responsibilities of parents and their children in the following passages:

    Colossians 3:20-21 _____

    Hebrews 12:5-11 _____

    Proverbs 3:11-12 _____

    Ephesians 6:4 _____

15. What kind of instruction and training should we be giving our children?

    _____

D. Financial Goals

1. Do you think I handle money properly?

   _____

2. How could I better manage our money?

   _____

3. Do you think I am:

   too frugal? _____

   too extravagant? _____

   about right? _____

   why? _____

4. Do you think I accept financial responsibilities well?

   _____

5. Do you think we communicate financial goals well?

_____

6. What is your immediate financial goal?

_____

7. What is your primary goal for this year?

_____

8. What is your plan for our children's education?

_____

9. What is your retirement goal?

_____

10. What do you think about tithing?

   Is tithing necessary? _____

   How much? _____

   Where should it go? _____

11. How do you feel about giving in general?

_____

12. Do you like the way we live?

_____

13. What changes would you like to see?

_____

Budget Problems Analysis

BOOKKEEPING ERRORS

In order to maintain an orderly budget, it is necessary to keep records. Those include both the previously established home budget and adequate bank records. Many people fail to exercise control over their checking accounts and seldom or never balance their records. It is impossible to balance a home budget without balancing your checking account. Go to your bank account manager, and ask his help if you cannot balance your records. Some helpful hints for this area are:

1. Use a ledger-type checkbook (as opposed to a stub type).

2. List all check numbers before writing the first check.

3. Record every check in the ledger immediately, in detail.

4. Only one person should keep the ledger and checkbook.

5. Balance the ledger every month.

HIDDEN DEBTS

These include bills that may not come due on a monthly basis. Nevertheless your budget must provide for them; failure to do so will frustrate your efforts to be a good steward.

Some debts of this type might include:

1. Tapes, books, and magazines
2. Retail outlet stores credit
3. Family, friends
4. Doctor, dentist
5. Taxes
6. Yearly insurance premiums

IMPULSE ITEMS

Impulse buying is common to most of us. A list of impulse purchases can range from homes, cars, and expensive trips to tools and entertainment items. The value is not the issue; the necessity is. Consider every purchase in light of your budgeted items, and avoid buying anything on impulse.

Some hints to reduce impulse buying:

1. Use a delayed purchase plan. Buy nothing that is outside your budget unless you wait thirty days.

2. During those thirty days, determine to find at least two items similar to the one you want to purchase to compare prices.

3. Allow only one new purchase at a time that is not part of your planned budget.

4. Never use credit cards for impulse purchases.

5. Stay out of the stores!

GIFTS

Gifts can jeopardize a budget quickly. Begin to seek alternatives for costly gifts both with your family and your friends. Regardless of your financial status, determine to bring this area under control. Following are some hints:

1. Keep an event calendar during the year, and plan ahead.

2. Initiate some family crafts, and make the gifts you need, such as wall plaques, knickknacks, purses, and string art. Not only do these make good gifts, but they reflect effort and love.

3. Draw family names for selected gifts rather than each family member giving to everyone.

4. Do not buy gifts on credit.

5. Help your children earn money for gifts.

6. Send cards on special birthdays and anniversaries.

Other Materials by Larry Burkett:

Books in this series:

Financial Freedom
Sound Investments
Major Purchases
Insurance Plans
Giving and Tithing
Personal Finances

Other Books:

Debt-Free Living
Financial Planning Workbook
How to Manage Your Money
Your Finances in Changing Times

Videos:

Your Finances in Changing Times
Two Masters
How to Manage Your Money
The Financial Planning Workbook

Other Resources:

Financial Planning Organizer
Debt-Free Living Cassette